Intersections:

Exploring Exclusion within Women's Only Protest Events

Caitlin Powell

An imprint of Boom Publications Ltd

272 Bath Street
Glasgow SCOTLAND
G2 4JR

We plant a tree for every
Boom Graduate book commissioned, and
thereafter plant a tree for every 10 books sold.

THG

(more : trees)

MEMBER

Watch our forest grow at
https://moretrees.eco/forest/BoomPublicationsLtd/

Intersections: Exploring Exclusion within Women's Only Protest Events

Contents

Author biography

Caitlin Powell is an intersectional feminist author, primarily focussing their research on protest events. She holds a First-class Honours degree in Creative Events Management from Arts University Bournemouth. After attending their first *Reclaim the Night* march as a teenager, Caitlin developed a keen interest in exploring feminist protest. As something that struck her both politically and personally, she wanted to understand the real stories of the forgotten feminist movements. What followed was nearly five years of sitting on various Feminist Society committees, as well as becoming the Gender Equalities Officer for her university. Visiting protest exhibitions across the UK and US, their affinity with the subject only grew. Caitlin has since graduated and is working in sustainability communications whilst exploring her research endeavours by taking part in local community action groups and seeking out new protest exhibitions wherever possible. Outside of work, Caitlin enjoys ballet, modern and tap dancing, sea swimming, visiting local museums and galleries, and a plethora of gigs and festivals.

Abstract

This book is a must-read for event planners who are looking to create more inclusive events, offering practical solutions and real-life examples. Drawing inspiration from talking to women who lived at Greenham Common, visiting the Still I Rise exhibition at the Arnolfini Gallery and – more broadly - intersectionality studies, the contextual analysis from this text has allowed for a critical evaluation of an eclectic mix of women's only protest events. This book focusses heavily on two events; Greenham Common Women's Peace Protest and Statement Festival to serve as a comparison for the ways in which internal and external factors from 1980's to 2010's have impacted exclusion. This is explored through the lens of the barriers faced by disabled women, women from lower socio-economic backgrounds, Black, Asian, and other ethnic minority women, non-binary and transgender people and the intersections between these inequalities.

Contrary to a hegemonic retelling of the history of women's only events, which presumed a white-led movement that chose to ignore their Black, disabled and gender-non-conforming counterparts; this book explores the real movements that took place.

Introduction

In a world before the word intersectionality, a term coined by Kimberlé Crenshaw in 1991 to define 'social justice problems, such as racism and sexism are overlapping to create multiple levels of social injustice' (Crenshaw, 2016), women's only protest events were subject to an unconscious bias.

Intersectionality refers to how race, ethnicity, gender, religion/creed, generation, geographic location, sexuality, age, ability/disability, and class intersect to shape the experiences of individuals; that identity is multidimensional. These identities are not mutually exclusive but interdependent (Bowleg, 2008).

The concept of unconscious bias occurs from an internalised prejudice of which the culprit is unaware. Thus, leading to engagement in discriminatory behaviour without conscious intent (Pritlove et al., 2019). 'It is clear that biases have the potential to impair rather than improve the quality of decisions' (Gvozdanović, 2018), therefore, the impact of exclusion at women's only protest events could be heightened by unconscious biases. This book will explore to what extent unconscious bias has played a role in excluding minorities from these events.

Second wave feminism, which spanned the 1960s, 70s and 80s, saw women fighting against remaining legal inequalities, for increased equality in family life, reproductive rights, domestic violence, sexism in popular culture and in the workplace– following the shift in occupational roles of men and women due to the disruption caused by the two World Wars (Grayzel, 2014).

Greenham Common Women's Peace Camp at its infancy was a Second Wave protest which entered into the Third Wave of feminism around 1990. Third Wave feminism aimed to develop and critique the work of First and Second Wave feminists using a 'tactical approach' (Snyder, 2008). Third Wave feminists used personal narratives in order to create intersectionality within their protests; embraced action amongst its members over theoretical justifications; and emphasised inclusivity through its refusal to create boundaries within protest events and the movement itself (Snyder, 2008).

Fourth Wave feminism has been heavily contested (Phillips and Cree, 2014). The resurgence of interest in feminism, materialised by Fourth

Wave feminists, can be characterised by its strong ties to consumerism in the Global North (Evans and Chamberlain, 2014).

The hegemonic retelling of Second Wave feminist history favouring white, middle-class, cisgender, able-bodied women is problematic when endeavouring to write an account of women's only events, as the majority of information is unreliable due to the clear bias. This book will analyse women's only protest events, starting with women's only organisations in the US from 1960 to 1980, then Greenham Common Women's Peace Camp from 1981 to 2000. The *Statement Festival* will also be analysed as an example of women's only protest in Fourth Wave feminism so as to provide a reference for how intersectionality has had an impact on exclusion in feminist organising. This book will determine the events in terms of exclusion towards marginalised groups – categorised by race, class, disability, sexuality and gender – and whether this has changed over time.

The second and third chapters of this book have been categorised by the case studies of two women's only protest events as opposed to categorising by oppression for two main reasons. Firstly, there is a disparity in the literature on the outlined marginalised communities being analysed within this book, which would make the chapters unevenly weighted. Secondly, separating the chapters by oppression does not acknowledge the multiplicity of inequalities faced by marginalised women which is outlined by Kimberlé Crenshaw in her work on intersectionality (Cho, Crenshaw and McCall, 2013). In such a short book, it is difficult to present a rounded view of each oppression. For this reason, there has been a clear focus on the issues of race and gender within this book, with other feminist issues being raised throughout such as class, disability, and sexuality.

The impacts of exclusion in women's only protest events can be measured along two axes, according to Spracklen (2015). Firstly, scale, which defines the range in size from small protests designed to challenge local issues to larger scale events which tackle systematic inequalities such as sexism, racism and class barriers. The second axis is content, which refers to the rationale behind the protests as well as the development of occurrences within the protest.

The acknowledgement of interlocking inequalities also plays an important role in measuring the impact of a women's only protest event. Women at the intersection of poverty and racism face high rates of incarceration, police brutality, joblessness, dislocation caused by urban renewal and inadequate public services (Valk, 2010). These challenges are acknowledged within the intersectionality framework, which makes the concept invaluable in women's only events in Fourth Wave feminism.

When collecting evidence of exclusion in women's only protest events, the author chose to use findings from three countries – U.S, U.K and Sweden. All three are countries who have embraced equality legislation, and all three cultures have been at the forefront of women's equality since the beginning of the women's movement (Binnard, 2017; Salam, 2019). To an extent, there are problems with limiting the findings to just three countries. There are many European countries which could have been included, for example France, which – as a counter to the countries chosen – appear to be somewhat lacking in the fight for equality (Thelocal.fr, 2019). The challenges have been somewhat mitigated through the considerations that have come into selecting these locations. The first consideration is that the U.K and U.S are both English speaking countries, limiting the risk of errors in translation – with Sweden being added as it was host to the Statement Festival which received a lot of English media coverage (O'Reilly, 2019). Secondly and most importantly, the argument of this book has been led by the events within their respective movements, rather than the context of the location.

Radical feminism is a recurring theme throughout this book. Radical feminism involves 'sexism, views of the superiority of women over men, and the goal to establish a separate world without men, a gynocracy' (Shibles, 1989). The topic has been raised by Thompson (2002), who comments that the rise of radical feminism is linked to the creation of anti-patriarchy organisations such as *Redstockings*, *Radicalesbians* and *Women's International Conspiracy from Hell* (WITCH), and the term is generally only attributed to white anti-patriarchy feminists. This topic will be further explored in order to determine whether this terminology has had an impact on the exclusion felt by minorities at women's only protest events.

Political Lesbianism, practiced by groups, such as Radicalesbians during the 1980's and later adopted by some residents at Greenham Common Women's Peace Camp, was used to 'legitimise lesbianism as visible, integrated love of women and, therefore, of oneself' (Phelan, 1993). This framework adapts the well-known principle 'the personal is political', coined by Carol Hanisch in

1969 (Lee, 2007), and clarifies a connection between itself and radical feminism in that both movements advocate for separation of women and men. Both groups are also historically opposed to transgender identities which will be explored with reference to the women's only protest groups outlined in this essay.

The understanding that inequalities are not mutually exclusive began entering feminist consciousness in the 1960s, proven through the founding of women's caucuses in the *Student Non-violent Co-ordinating Committee* (SNCC) in the early 1960s and autonomous feminist groups such as *Women of All Red Nations* in 1974. Despite this, the term 'intersectionality' was only coined in 1991 by Kimberlé Crenshaw, which is defined by McCall as 'the most important theoretical contribution of feminism to date' (McCall, 2005). Intersectionality is described by Jorba and Rodó-Zárate as 'a framework that is able to recognise the complex ways in which inequalities are enmeshed' (Jorba and Rodó-Zárate, 2019). Intersectionality can be used as a defining characteristic of anti-racist feminist groups of Second Wave feminism. The key texts used in the first chapter are Re-visioning the Women's Liberation Movement's Narrative: Early Second Wave African American Feminists (Baxandall, 2001) and Multiracial Feminism: Recasting the Chronology of Second Wave Feminism (Thompson, 2002). These are both examples of anti-racist feminist historians whose work aims to reset the chronology of Second Wave feminism to include the stories of black women and other oppressed communities.

The interview participant wishes to be referred to as *Ray* within the context of this book. A full transcript of email correspondence can be found in appendix one. This will comprise the key text for the second chapter, alongside the public lecture Greenham Women Everywhere attended by the author in December 2019.

The third and final chapter explores exclusion within the women's only protest event, Statement Festival. The impacts will be measured against the aforementioned parameters of Second, Third and Fourth Wave feminism, as well as intersectionality framework.

This book will conclude with some recommendations for industry on how to continue more inclusively and ensure that the impact of exclusion is minimised for future women's only protest events. The primary aim of this book is to develop knowledge of underrepresented elements of women's only protest events. This will be achieved through a mixture of primary and secondary research, with a focus on academic journals from anti-racist feminist historians.

To some extent, this book is centred around the gaps that have been found in the mainstream understanding of women's only protest events. This book aims to evaluate the current literature available and bring new evidence forward using primary research.

Chapter One:

Contextual Analysis of Second Wave Feminism and Women's Only Protests

Feminist academics such as Rosalyn Baxandall state that contributions by black and anti-racist feminists have been retrospectively written out of Second Wave history by authors such as Sheila Tobias (1998), despite evidence that black and other ethnic minority women played a vital role in the organising of the women's liberation movement. As Elizabeth Toledo comments, "Women of colour have shaped the feminist movement from inception in this country [US], yet the public face of feminism is often seen as white" (Toledo, 1998). This is contrary to the popular notion that white middle-class women started the women's liberation movement and proceeded to exclude black and other ethnic minority women. The same is true for contributions from poor women, lesbians, transgender women and disabled women since 1960. This chapter will therefore comprise a brief retrospective telling of Second Wave feminist history using anti-racist feminist theorists such as Angela Davis, Becky Thompson and Rosalyn Baxandall. Using these academic sources will exhibit how the voices of black, brown and indigenous women, poor women, disabled women and transgender women have been erased from feminist discourse in Second Wave feminism and aim to highlight the experiences of these women in protest.

Black feminist and academic Barbara Smith set up the *Combahee River Collective* in 1974 - a black lesbian organisation inspired by the National Black Feminist Organisation formed to address the needs of its members which were not being addressed through the Civil Rights Movement. The Combahee River Collective also introduced the terms 'interlocking oppressions' and 'identity politics' into anti-racist feminism (Taylor, 2019). Six years later, she founded *Kitchen Table Women of Colour Press* (Smith, 1989) which was designed to air frustrations with white feminism which holds sexism as the ultimate oppression and ignores a class and race analysis in favour of an individual rights-based goal. Informed by Smith, in her writing Thompson (2002) uses the term 'anti-patriarchy' when referring to white feminist activist groups of the Second Wave movement.

'Anti-patriarchy' feminism refers to the work of radical feminists such as academic and author of

The Female Eunuch, Germaine Greer (1970), which places equality with men as the central cause. This book will refer to these "radical" feminists as anti-patriarchy feminists and white feminists interchangeably so as to avoid listing the minorities which were not included in their single focus approach to gender equality.

Women's only protest events, much like the movements behind them, have generally grown from other social justice causes. When looking at "radical" feminism, which is a driving force of women's only protest events, the two roots are widely considered to be the *Civil Rights Movement*, and *New Left ideologies* (Evans, 1979). Of course, this is combined with the notion that the term 'radical' has generally only been attributed to white feminists such as Andrea Dworkin and Catherine MacKinnon by mainstream Second Wave historians, like the radical lesbian feminist and author of *The Church and the Second Sex Mary Daly* (1968). It appears that an approach to feminism which includes attention to race, class and imperialism does not qualify anti-racist feminists such as Anna Mae Aquash, Marilyn Buck, or Laura Whitehorn to be defined as "radical" (Thompson, 2002). This trajectory completely omits the impact of the Black Power Movement on women's activism. Therefore, it fails to acknowledge the multiplicity of inequalities faced by women of colour, and other oppressed minorities including poor, transgender and disabled women.

Contesting the definition of "radical" brings to light new evidence which could suggest a rationale for the overlooking of contributions by women of colour by Second Wave historians. Anti-patriarchy feminism has prevailed as the dominant narrative of Second Wave history which could partly be attributed to hesitation amongst women of colour to use the term "feminist" for fears of being linked to white, anti-patriarchal feminism. Black and anti-racist feminists have referred to themselves as "woman-ist", "radical women of colour", and "social activists", which designates this activism with women at its core to not be included in what Sherna Berger Gluck termed 'the master historical narrative' (Naples, 2012). This fails to account for activism which was carried out by women of colour in mixed gender organisations and feminist work which represented women at the intersections of multiple inequalities.

Multi-racial feminist groups of the 1970s challenged inequality on a three-pronged basis – 'working with white-dominated feminist groups, forming women's caucuses in existing mixed-gender organisations, and developing autonomous Black, Latina, Native American, and Asian feminist organisations' (Thompson, 2002). This therefore, proves that feminist protest by women of colour which extends beyond women-only spaces has largely been ignored by the hegemonic retelling of Second Wave history through authors such as Barbara Ryan (1992).

The multi-racial feminist movement in the United States in the 1960s to 1980s can identify its roots to three social justice causes; the Civil Rights Movement, New Left ideologies and the Black Power Movement which have ultimately produced three groups of "radical" feminists. It is evident from these contributing groups that anti-racist feminism had a clear understanding of other social factors which affect women. These mixed-gender, nationalist organisations were also instrumental in the formation of the structure of anti-racist women's only organisations such as *Women of All Red Nations* (WARN), *Asian Sisters*, *Hijas de Cuauhtemoc* and *Third World Women's Alliance* (1968) which all adopted the strategy of appointing officers to fill specific roles (Josephy, 1999: p. 52).

Through researching the roots of the Women's Liberation Movement and the protest events held within it, it is apparent that there is a gap in the literature on this subject. There are very few historical studies dedicated to the Women's Liberation Movement, and much less on the experiences of black and anti-racist feminists of this time, 'because the Women's Liberation Movement was so decentralised, finding information often requires interviewing participants and digging into personal papers and local libraries' (Baxandall, 2001). Instead, scholars in contemporary feminism focus their studies on liberal organisations such as the pressure group *National Organisation for Women* (NOW) as it has been better documented through minutes of their meetings. Contrary to these organisations whose members were predominantly professional women who kept a paper trail of their meetings and events in published writings, the anti-racist feminists associated with the *Women's Liberation Movement*, such as the *National Black Feminist Organisation*, *Women of All Red Nations* and the *Combahee River Collective*, operated informally. Generally, publications produced by groups or individuals in the women's liberation movement would be left unsigned and not dated, here Baxandall provides four possible explanations for this phenomenon, perhaps because we lacked a sense of our own history and importance, lived in the present, felt all property (even intellectual property) was theft, and desired all or no-one to be stars. (Baxandall, 2001)

These reasons can be further explained by the movement's strong links to New Left ideologies. Membership in the women's liberation movement was assumed through the attendance of events and consciousness raising groups, there was no leadership due to an express resistance to operating with a rigid hierarchy, such as their male counterparts in organisations such as the Old Left, from which many of the early Women's Liberation Movement groups formed (Thompson, 2002).

In the absence of leaders within the Women's Liberation Movement, informal communication methods, such as the production of pamphlets, t-shirts, songs, posters and badges provided a "common culture" between the various groups within the movement. Despite considering themselves separate entities with no formal connections, their views and aims often aligned. Women's only protest groups could be characterised by their common culture, adding to inclusivity felt by minorities within these organisations. These were the most popular methods of communication as the Women's Liberation Movement was one of the last before the invention of the internet, which has inevitably reduced unconscious bias by making information more readily available.

The protest events which shaped the Women's Liberation Movement were sporadic and often disjointed as 'groups frequently sprang up without formal connections to others' (Baxandall, 2001: p. 226). The memo *Sex and Caste* (Hayden and King, 1965) contained notes between the two former Student, Non-violent, Co-ordinating

Committee members and is held as the 'start' of the Women's Liberation Movement. As a grassroots movement, it is difficult to determine the defining moments which 'started' the movement as 'the opening moves take place in streets, living rooms and churches...' (Baxandall, 2001).

Mainstream historical accounts of Second Wave Feminism, described by Chela Sandoval as 'hegemonic feminism' (Sandoval, 2000), such as Alice Echol's *Daring to be Bad: Radical Feminism in America, 1967 – 1975* (1989), paint a picture of women's only events of the 1960s and 1970s which was white, middle class, cisgender and able-bodied. The widely considered catalysts of Second Wave feminism in the United States are attributed to the publication of Betty Friedan's *The Feminine Mystique* (1963), the founding of the National Organisation for Women (NOW) in 1966 and the development of 'consciousness raising' groups – pioneered by *New York Radical Women* (NYRW) in 1967 (Thompson, 2002). Juxtaposing mainstream feminism with the achievements of the anti-racist movement highlights the popularly disputed contention of what constitutes liberation. From an anti-racist perspective, liberation is only achieved when all intersections of oppressed identities are liberated, whereas the single focus approach of white feminism denotes that liberation is achieved when the rights of women are equal to the rights of men. A retrospective retelling of Second Wave history to include contributions by black and anti-racist women, poor women, transgender and non-binary people and disabled feminists aims to disarm the misconception that Second Wave feminists with multiple inequalities used the anti-patriarchy feminist movement as a tool to inform their reactionary causes.

Hayden and King (1965), provided an explanation in their private memo Sex and Caste for the erasure of the work of anti-racist and poor women throughout the 1960s, which was circulated by Liberation Magazine; Objectively, the chances seem nil that we could start a movement based on anything as distant to general American thought as a sex-caste system. Therefore, most of us will probably want to work full time on problems such as war, poverty, race… (Hayden and King, 1966).

This demonstrates a lack of understanding of the multiplicity of struggles faced by poor women and women of colour in America in the 1960s, and moreover highlights that mainstream feminism did not deem racism, imperialism nor poverty to be feminist issues. This is further evidenced by

Baxandall (2001: p. 241) who names autonomous black women's group Mothers Alone Working as an example of a group carrying out work in women's only space but were not acknowledged as feminist. Baxandall suggests that these women were ignored by writers and other media at the time on account of primarily being engaged in self-help and neighbourhood action, but mostly because they were viewed as organisations to aid poor women (2001). Placing these organisations through the parameters of intersectionality practiced in Fourth Wave feminism would qualify them as feminist, as well as an early example of feminist organising in protest against poverty and racism.

The juxtaposing timelines of hegemonic and multiracial feminism, created by Thompson, highlight a key difference in the organising of protest events during Second Wave feminism, that black and anti-racist feminism existed in more diverse spaces than that of its white counterpart. The timelines also challenge the notion that black feminism was set up as a reactionary cause to, and therefore later than, white feminism. They prove that the timing of black feminist organising, as asserted by Benita Roth in her critique of 'reductive' model making, is roughly on par with their white counterparts (Roth, 2004). This is also true of Native American, Latina and Asian American feminist organisations.

The ideology of anti-racist feminism was committed to continuous change and growth in order to remain inclusive. This is evidenced through the adaptation of the well-known principle 'The Personal Is Political' to 'The Personal is Political and the Political Is Personal' by anti-racist feminist Anne Braden (1999). This highlights the experiences of marginalised women in protest as their lives are continually politicised, and also challenges anti-racist feminists to ensure that political issues 'need to be personally committed to – whether you have been victimised by those issues or not' (Thompson, 2002: p 347).

Despite the *Disability Rights Movement* following roughly the same timeline as Second Wave feminism, it appears to be continually disregarded in intersectionality studies. In order to remain relevant, women's only events must show an understanding of disability within their intersectionality.

The protest event, *New York Women Against Rape Conference* in 1984 demonstrates an acknowledgement of intersectionality during Second Wave feminism, as the women's only event was said to have 'confronted multiple challenges facing women organising against violence against women – by partners, police, social service agencies and poverty' (Thompson, 2002). The acknowledgement of intertwining oppressions plays an important role in analysing the impact of women's only protest events. On this scale, the extent to which the New York Women Against Rape Conference focuses on the issue of women in poverty concludes that there is an awareness of class-based prejudices within feminism, creating an inclusive space for working-class women and women of colour. However, the issues of gender and disability as contributing factors to sex-based prejudice are not included as a focus of the event, highlighting that there are still missing elements which would help to minimise the negative impacts of exclusion on this women's-only protest event.

Women's only events in Second Wave feminism moved towards collective creation of art – with a focus on creating 'women-centric art' which was salient in a male-dominated art world. The fight was not simply for women artists to be seen, but to lay foundations for a new kind of art making that stepped away from ideas of the lone male genius and his proprietorial dominance over the natural world (Judah, 2019).

The art created was also used as a device with which to address issues raised by Second Wave feminism, qualifying it as a means of protest (Kelly and Breinlinger, 1995). However, critics of this art movement, such as Esther Allen, have since questioned the mainstream feminist art collectives of this era as they appear to have overlooked key aspects of feminism addressed by intersectionality (Allen, 2018).

Feminist art critics stated that there was little female representation within the arts industry. Frustrations rose as the Art Workers Coalition were unwilling to protest on behalf of women or other marginalised groups. This culminated in 1969 when New York women left the coalition and went on to form the group Women Artists in Revolution (WAR), which campaigned for the inclusion of women artists in galleries such as the Whitney Museum of American Art (Swartz, 2011). By 1970, the protests by WAR had garnered so much attention that the percentage of female artists exhibited at the Whitney had increased to 23%, compared to just 10% the previous year (Ristanovic, 2019). The representation of female artists in galleries was a positive step towards inclusion in Second Wave feminism. However, the unconscious bias facing WAR prevented them from viewing the inequalities faced by other women at the intersections of multiple oppressions.

Women's only protest in this sphere had been heavily influenced by white feminist artists such as Hannah Wilke, a New York sculptor and performance artist whose work confronted typical notions of sexuality and femininity. Her most well-known work *S.O.S – Starification Object Series* (1974 – 82) features depictions of the female genitalia, which by Fourth Wave standards, could be construed as an example of trans-exclusionary radical feminism. The introduction of intersectionality into Third and Fourth Wave feminism comes with an understanding that gender is a social construct, and that not all women have vulvas (Wenzlaff, Briken and Dekker, 2018). However, unconscious bias has had a clear role to play in this piece of work, as the impact of exclusion felt by transgender women is more widely acknowledged in Fourth Wave feminism than when the art was created. Thus, the question needs to be raised; does a lack of inclusion equal exclusion?

Another notable culprit of this unconscious bias is Judy Chicago's installation piece – The Dinner Table, which was originally exhibited in 1974(Chicago, 2018). Despite being regarded as the first epic feminist artwork (Gotthardt, 2018), there have since been issues raised with the installation artwork, which contains representations of 39 mythical and historical women (Weber, 2018).

Firstly, the large-scale exclusion of women of colour within Chicago's work could be acknowledged as an unconscious bias. Esther Allen notes in *Returning the Gaze: With a Vengeance* that 'It's now quite hard to keep from noticing that none of the thirty-nine Great Women granted a place at Chicago's elaborate table is from Spain, Portugal, or any of those empires' former colonies in the Americas (Allen, 2018)'.

Chicago responded to the criticism from Allen stating that 'At the time I was working on The Dinner Party, in the mid-1970s, there was little or no knowledge about any of these women' (Weber, 2018). This response highlights how bias affects the judgement of the work of Second Wave feminists through the lens of Third and Fourth Wave understanding. The impact of intersectionality on feminism is clearly construed here by the juxtaposition from the mid-1970s to 2018 in our understandings of race and the ways in which inequalities are compounded for women of colour.

In her work *Test plates for The Dinner Party* (1974-1979), Judy Chicago uses iconography to challenge traditional gender roles but does little to acknowledge transgender women. The depictions of vulvas to represent women is an example of how a lack of inclusion has denoted exclusion towards transgender women. This raises a further question; are a lack of inclusion and direct exclusion are equal in their impacts? Understandings of gender have largely shifted from a binary construct to a fluid spectrum of gender identities. Therefore, the impact of indirect exclusion towards transgender women has increased as our understanding has developed.

The collective element of the women's only creation of art gave a rationale for women's only spaces in protest within Second Wave feminism. In a similar manner to the organisation of women-centric art in a male dominated industry, women continued to group together to protest patriarchal values upheld by society in the 1970s.

Thus far this book has argued that exclusion within women's only protest events in Second Wave feminism was not as commonplace as the hegemonic retelling of its history. Women of colour were protesting at the same time as anti-patriarchy feminists and arguably, in more diverse spaces. Mainstream history, however, has contrived a narrative whereby anti-patriarchy feminists started a movement to which black and anti-racist feminists contributed very little, and much later. The work of feminist historians such as Baxandall, Davis and Thompson have challenged these notions, which has in turn, paved the way to reduce the impact of exclusion in future women's only protest events.

The external factor of unconscious bias was the most common justification for exclusion within white feminist spheres and manifested in the exclusion of women from a range of marginalised backgrounds, including women of colour, poor women, transgender and women with disabilities. This was perpetuated by a distinct difference in access to information between Second Wave and today, as the internet has exponentially grown feminist consciousness (Clark, 2007).

Chapter Two

Greenham Common Women's Peace Camp; 1981-2000

In the summer of 1981, tensions grew to new heights among peace activists surrounding the heavily contested placement of U.S nuclear weapons on British soil. Greenham Common, a former Air Force base situated in Newbury used for the U.S deployment of cruise missiles, soon became home to one of the first and longest-standing women's only protests the UK had ever seen. Greenham Common Women's Peace Camp remained a site of protest for nearly twenty years. It became home to women around the world and represented a new landscape of feminist protest events. This chapter seeks to assess the extent to which Greenham Common Women's Peace Camp was exclusionary, through the lenses of class, race, ability, gender, and sexuality. Thus, the first element to explore must be the roots of the protest.

The root of the protest is relatively clear from an anti-militarist and environmental standpoint, the camp started as a campaign against nuclear weapons which later developed into challenging 'the patriarchal traditions and symbols that the missiles represented' (Laware, 2004: p 1). Environmental activism provides an explanation for the root of many women's only protest events and Greenham Common Women's Peace Camp is no exception. The environmental content of this women's only protest leans itself towards the categorisation of 'ecofeminism'. Ecofeminism emerged from the intersections of feminist research and the various movements for social justice and environmental health, explorations that uncovered the linked oppressions of gender, ecology, race, species and nation (Gaard, 2011).

This definition suggests a link between intersectionality and environmental feminist protest. Intersectionality studies also connote an understanding that oppressions facing women such as poverty and racism are exacerbated by one another. In turn, this leads to environmental impacts disproportionately affecting marginalised women in our society (Hamilton, 2019). For instance, substantially higher exposure to air pollution within poor communities (Katz, 2012). This would lead one to believe that this protest, stemming from an environmental cause, would have a firm grasp of the impact of exclusion felt by minorities. This chapter will assess to what extent the Greenham Common Women's Peace Camp engaged and represented these marginalised women within the protest.

The women's only protest was originally accessible to men and women. The camp was established from a spontaneous idea formed by the group *Women for Life on Earth* on their nine-day peace march from Cardiff to Greenham Common in Berkshire, which included four men. The decision came a few months after the initial march, and signs were posted around the camp with the words "Women's Peace Camp", condemning the male supporters of the protest to leave the site and only return during daylight, and not as permanent residents of the peace camp (Laware, 2004). Anecdotal evidence from the event Greenham Women Everywhere, a public lecture given by Rebecca Morden and Ray – two women who lived at the camp, divulged that some of the women jokingly referred to their male supporters as "the sandwich makers" (Morden and Ray, 2019). This decision changed the direction of the protest and ultimately blurred the lines of context in terms of its relevance as a women's only event. The camp was also divergent in its inception, not only because it started as a mixed-gender organisation, but because it was not primarily formed as a political reaction to patriarchal control. Many women's only spaces throughout Second Wave history were formed as a reaction to sexual violence or other challenges disproportionately affecting women. However, it was joked by Ray – a permanent resident of the peace camp – that the reasoning behind making Greenham Common a women's only camp was 'because the men wouldn't do the bloody washing up' (Raymond, 2019).

Feminist artwork, such as Rehana Zaman's *Tell Me the Story of All These Things* (2017), demonstrates that women only spaces have an important role to play in sparking conversations surrounding the delicate subjects of domestic and sexual violence. Therefore, the creation of a women's only space at Greenham Common was conducive to challenging notions of patriarchal control. A growing importance was placed on the aspect of life as a woman at the camp. Challenging the patriarchal 'killing power of men and their war machines' (Ray, 2020) became a defining characteristic of this women's only protest. Although the camp was not originally intended as a feminist protest, the women were able to share their grievances with the male-dominated society they were living in. At the event Greenham Women Everywhere, Ray spoke about the women at camp slowly becoming comfortable with sharing personal stories of sexual trauma and domestic violence (2019). We began to understand why we might have food issues, self-harm, anxiety; we screamed at the planes and released our anger. We threw gloop at the convoys, banged drums and pans, it was very therapeutic to give vent to our suppressed anger in these ways (Ray, 2020).

Through the axis of content laid out by Spracklen and Lamond (2015), the safe space created for these Greenham women adds value and relevance to the women's only dimension of the protest. The impact of exclusion towards minorities was lessened in this way by the Greenham residents, a lot of work was achieved through conversation due to its completely non-violent nature (Morden and Ray, 2019).

Separatist feminism, which was on the rise in the 1980s in the UK, is described as 'the belief that women must and should be separate from men politically and personally in order to accomplish the goals of a feminist revolution' (Shugar, 1995). Separatist feminism and its advocacy for the total separation of men and women demonstrates Greenham Common as an example of separatism in protest. The 'separatist' phenomenon was an important driving force for women's only protest during Second Wave feminism, shaping the course of the feminist movement for the 20th Century (McGarry and Wasserman, 1998).

As with all movements, and the events within them, the content of Greenham Common Women's Peace Camp was continually shifting. 'Greenham had come to 'stand for' itself, a constantly changing terrain of women's symbolic protests and direct action' (Emberley and Landry, 1989: p 485). The separatist element of the protest allowed for conversation topics to evolve throughout the years of the camp. Many women who permanently lived at Greenham were not only sharing stories of sexual violence but sharing experiences of the police brutality and institutional state violence faced at Greenham. Through sharing experiences, the impact of exclusion towards marginalised women at Greenham grew smaller.

The women's discontent with being treated as second class citizens, a cornerstone of Second Wave feminist organising, had inevitably filtered into the conversations between the residents of the camp. Parts of life at the camp exacerbated their grievances; reproductive rights were high on the mainstream Second Wave feminist agenda. Ray, like many other Greenham women, has spoken about the police violence they faced; 'they experimented with Taser frequencies on us' (Morden and Ray, 2019). The women also discouraged pregnant women and women trying to conceive from coming to camp (Laware, 2004; Ray, 2020).

Ray comments that the main reason for a lack of representation of black and minority ethnic women at Greenham Common was largely due to police brutality. 'Some black women did come to Greenham but were targeted by racist Police and MoD police' (Ray, 2020). Sue Say, another Greenham woman, concurs with Ray and reflects in an interview with Evening Standard that she was 'put in handcuffs and guns were put to the back of my head' (O'Reilly, 2019). Some women from minority ethnic backgrounds also risked being alienated by their families and religious communities by working in a political capacity with white women (Ray, 2020). This adds another dimension to the debate of exclusion occurring at the women's only protest. While black and minority ethnic women were discouraged from coming to camp, this was not due to express exclusion by the protest event itself. Rather, the external factors of institutional state violence and societal norms proving to be the main culprits of exacerbating the exclusion felt by women of colour.

In the same vein as white feminist groups in the United States from 1960-80, Greenham women were averse to leadership because of their desire to cut ties with Old Left links (Thompson, 2002). This even went as far as organising the seven gates that lead into the base not by number, but by colour. Morden explained at Greenham Women Everywhere that this was another way in which the women were able to 'challenge patriarchal narratives' as this system avoided hierarchy (Morden and Ray, 2019). Each gate had its own characteristics, overall contributing to the inclusivity of the camp (appendix two). Greenham Common Women's Peace Camp, like the National Black Feminist Organisation and the Combahee River Collective, did not have a leader. Ray comments that 'we tried to not let the press isolate us by asking to speak to our "leader" with the response "we have no leaders here"' (Ray, 2020). As well as defying patriarchal narratives, this lessened the impact of exclusion as class difference would have impeded the ability of some working-class women to speak with confidence to the press. Middle-class "gatekeeping" of feminism has been a controversial topic amongst Third and Fourth Wave feminists, in relation to how academic language can dissuade working-class women from engaging with the feminist agenda (Cameron, 2002; Lewis, 2014). To a certain extent, Greenham Common limited the impact of exclusion felt by poor women by challenging patriarchal norms of leadership and allowing for every woman at camp to be heard.

When asked the question, 'what measures were put in place for poor women who wanted to protest at Greenham?', Ray responded that 'we were all poor!' (Ray, 2020). The women at Greenham Common worked hard to engage with poor women, shown through the 'camp dole' that was accessible in times of hardship (Morden and Ray, 2019; Ray, 2020). Other measures that were taken included organising food donations from the local community and accepting coal from miners (Laware, 2004; Morden and Ray, 2019; Ray, 2020).

From the perspective of working-class and poor women, there was a diverse range of representation and specific measures were taken by the women who lived at camp to ensure that Greenham Common was inclusive towards these women. Therefore, the impact of exclusion by Greenham Common Women's Peace Camp was minimal to this group.

Some members of the camp practiced Political Lesbianism as a form of interrogating the confining definitions of what it meant to be a woman, which challenged 'heterosexual women to extricate themselves from sexual and emotional ties to men' (Ray, 2020). Lesbian erasure is argued by Rayas the primary reason for the invisibility of Greenham Common Women's Peace Camp (Morden and Ray, 2019). Morden described this phenomenon as 'cultural robbery' and stated that 'no-one under thirty knows about Greenham, and anyone over thirty has an opinion on it' (Morden and Ray, 2019). In her interview, Ray commented that 'plenty of heterosexual peace activists wanted us lesbians to be invisible so as not to give the press another reason to dismiss us' (Ray, 2020). This begs the question; did the ways in which the media reported on Greenham have a direct impact on the inclusivity of the protest?

To draw a comparison between organising in the 1980s, and Third and Fourth Wave feminism; Greenham Common Women's Peace Camp can be likened to *Extinction Rebellion* activism (O'Reilly, 2019) when looking at how the two have been affected by biased reporting from the media. Many mainstream media outlets had compressed the Greenham Common Women's Peace Camp into a campaign of mothers protecting the earth for their children (Ray, 2020). While it was true that many women who lived at camp were mothers, this single story damaged the complex aims of the Greenham women, as well as invalidating the separatist and political roots of the protest, with Ray commenting that 'I found this annoying, reducing our activism to our function as mothers; I and many of us were there because of our concern over the destruction of nature which we saw as the arrogance of man' (Ray, 2020).

The overarching story of the concerned mother is one that still affects women's only protest today. This is exhibited by certain women's only factions of Extinction Rebellion being largely ignored by the media in favour of reports on splinter groups such as Mothers Rise Up and Parents for Future. This has reduced the involvement of women in Extinction Rebellion to only acknowledge mothers (ITV News, 2019; Jarvis, 2019; Duell, 2019). This is supported by Susan Bordo in her work Are Mothers Persons? in the book Unbearable Weight: Feminism, Western Culture and the Body (Bordo and Heywood, 2009), which examines the bodily autonomy of women and explores how 'women are re-imagined as mere carriers of foetuses' (Thornham, 2000: p 170).

Despite this, Extinction Rebellion has yet to be described as a feminist protest by the media. Intersectionality framework has taught modern feminists that challenges of racism, poverty, imperialism and climate change are feminist issues. To an extent, this developed understanding is not reflected by the media's reporting of Extinction Rebellion. By reducing this protest and Greenham Common Women's Peace Camp to campaigns by and for mothers, the media has helped to perpetuate the impact of exclusion felt by marginalised women as it fails to acknowledge the multiplicity of inequalities faced by these women which do not centre around their roles as mothers.

As explored in Feminist Disability Studies, this study will challenge the notion that disability is an inherent flaw, by highlighting the experiences of disabled women at Greenham Common Women's Peace Camp. Feminism challenges the belief that femaleness is a natural form of physical and mental deficiency or constitutional unruliness. Feminist Disability Studies similarly questions our assumptions that disability is a flaw, lack or excess (Garland-Thompson, 2005).

Feminist Disability Studies also seek to disarm the grouping together of disabilities as this adds to the impact of exclusion felt by women with disabilities. In this respect, Greenham Common

Women's Peace Camp has shown an awareness of disabled women's issues within intersectionality framework. In her interview (appendix one), Ray comments that the women used 'creative solutions' in order to support each other.

From the vantage point of accessibility at Greenham Common, there was somewhat of a lack of inclusion. Unconscious bias has had a clear role to play in this, and it could be argued that this lack of inclusion has equalled exclusion on this occasion as this would have prevented women with disabilities from coming to camp. There was no real representation nor forethought for accessibility due to the nature of the location; 'the common was rough terrain and we were squatters so we were very limited in terms of infrastructural adjustments; we constructed planks and tarps for wheelchair users, they only lasted until the bailiffs removed them' (Ray, 2020). This demonstrates exclusion on an institutional level as it highlights the efforts to be inclusive from the perspective of the women at the camp being dismantled by authority.

Much like race issues presented at Greenham Common, disabled women faced exclusion on a structural and institutional level. Whilst it is clear that this was not a priority of the Greenham Common protest, there were efforts made by the majority of women living at the camp to create an inclusive environment for women with disabilities.

Location is pertinent when exploring exclusion within women's only protest events. Greenham Common Women's Peace Camp signalled the reclamation of private space as political space, making the location a defining characteristic of the aims of the protest. The rural location could have excluded women with physical disabilities, as well as poor women who did not have access to transport. However, in her interview, Ray commented that Greenham was 'an international movement' (2020). This approach challenges notions of traditional protest by redefining the parameters of what it meant to be a Greenham woman.

'We did not consider it essential to actually be at camp, on the common, to be a "Greenham woman". Greenham women are everywhere was a 'meme'. You did not even need to live in the UK, we were an internationalist movement.' (Ray, 2020).

Wider external problems of institutional racism, ableism and societal norms have all held crucial roles in the impact of exclusion at Greenham Common Women's Peace Camp. These external factors largely discouraged women of colour from attending the protest. Although Greenham was a strictly non-violent protest, institutional state violence culminated in women of colour being disproportionately discriminated against by the police force and MoD police at Greenham Common.

Biased reporting within the media was also a clear external culprit of excluding minorities from Greenham Common Women's Peace Camp. The impact of exclusion in this way was felt mostly by transgender women. The understanding of a non-binary gender spectrum, at this time, was limited. Therefore, it could be said that the lack of inclusion within the protest was equal to exclusion, as a direct result of anti-patriarchy feminist views and media reporting at the time.

Chapter Three

Statement Festival 2018

The Statement Festival, founded by Emma Knyckare, first took place on 31st August and 1st September 2018 in Sweden. The festival was only open to a female, transgender and non-binary audience. Only female, transgender and non-binary artists were eligible to perform. The crew was mostly made up of female staff and the security staff were also almost all female-identifying (O'Connor, 2017).

Around 5,000 people attended the festival, when later that year it was announced that there would not be another due to a ruling by a Swedish court deeming the festival discriminatory towards men (O'Reilly, 2019). It was found by the *Swedish Equality Ombudsman*, four months after the event, that the Statement Festival had breached gender discrimination laws by explicitly stating that it was a 'man-free' festival, allowing only 'women, transgender and non-binary people' (Hooton, 2018). This direct exclusion, however, did not adversely impact any men as they were not prohibited from buying tickets to the event, nor were any men turned away from the event. The question then leads on to asking, were any marginalised groups impacted by exclusion at the Statement Festival?

The Statement Festival can be defined as a protest event as new understandings by 'social movement theorists have recognized the significance of movement cultural politics, new approaches are needed to understand the carnivalesque character of the contemporary activism' (St John, 2008). The festival also aligns with Taylor, Rupp and Gamson's theoretical definition of protest in Performing Protest: Drag Shows as Tactical Repertoire of the Gay and Lesbian Movement (2004). The term 'tactical repertoires' was coined by Taylor, Rupp and Gamson to mean events which are representative of the movements behind them. They have identified three elements of tactical repertoires; 'contestation, intentionality, and collective identity' (2004). The Statement Festival acts as a tactical repertoire for the feminist movement in all three elements.

The elements of 'contestation' and 'intentionality' are clearly shown through the inception of the event, which challenged the sensitive topic of sexual assault at festivals. The

Statement Festival was launched as a reaction to Sweden's largest festival, *Bravalla*, reporting increasing amounts of rape cases at the festival year on year. Bravalla festival was cancelled in 2018 due to these reported cases (Halpin, 2017). This validates the 'contestation' element of the protest event, in that the festival's inception was a response to these violent acts. In this way, the festival acts as a safe space for victims of sexual trauma which highlights the 'intentionality' behind the festival and minimises the impact of exclusion. This was achieved in the same manner as conversations about sensitive topics at Greenham Common mentioned in the second chapter of this book.

'Collective identity' was demonstrated by the attendance of the event by 5,000 women, transgender and non-binary people. Opposing critics such as the Deviant Developer (2020), this chapter argues that there is a need for women's only spaces in certain contexts. This is demonstrated by the success of the Statement Festival. In the context of women opening up about trauma they have faced at the hands of men, such as the Greenham women talking about domestic violence (Morden and Ray, 2019), a space away from men is relevant. Context is perhaps the most salient point to examine in determining the relevance of women's only protest events.

Craig Robertson states in Protests as Events that the songs used in protest movements 'provided an amplification system for communication purposes' and described the music of movements such as the Civil Rights Movement as 'the scaffolding on which to hang certain messages' (Spracklen and Lamond, 2015: p 180). The Statement Festival demonstrated this by using music as a form of communicating the message of the festival.

The commodification of music within the Civil Rights Movement, while propagating the cause, led to a number of supporters feeling as though they had become part of the movement solely by purchasing physical copies of the music (Spracklen and Lamond, 2015). The same could be said for the crowdfunding supporters of the Statement Festival, who collectively raised 533,120SEK (£46,555) in order to launch the festival (Snapes, 2018). It is clear that the festival achieved its aim of propagating a message of support for sexual assault victims, however this expression of support could also connote weak participation. The impact of exclusion is increased by this as it sends a message to working class women that capital is a primary way to show dedication to the cause.

Mainstream Fourth Wave feminism also operates with a seemingly class-based hierarchy due to its intrinsic links to capitalism. The commodification of feminism in recent years as it has increased in popularity, has been a hotly debated topic (Dowsett, 2014; Shane, 2018). While the economic success of the festival represents the need for events such as this, the impact of exclusion is felt by working class women who have been met by a barrier to entry through the price of the festival tickets. This type of exclusion is indirect as the price is clearly representative of the costs of running the festival. However, this highlights a lack of class-based analysis by the Statement Festival as no direct measures were taken to limit the impact of this exclusion.

Opposition to capitalism is a clear directive of socialist feminism, which has been criticised for putting too much emphasis on class-based divides (Aschoff, 2016). Many feminists agree with the notion that there can be no feminism under capitalism due to the structural imbalances caused by capitalism, not just in the Global North. This challenges mainstream Fourth Wave feminist outlooks on the commodification of and participation in women's only events, which have been deemed as 'performative' (Sharma, 2018). The popularity of women's only events in Fourth Wave feminism has widened a class-based gap within mainstream feminism as the economic power of the female market has given way to the movement becoming consumer centric. This, in turn, indirectly excludes working class women.

Angie Ng in Protests as Events highlights a counter argument to the traditional feminist opposition of capitalism by commenting, 'if progressive social movements wish to have coverage, they must have some "selling points"' (Spracklen and Lamond, 2015: p 50). Coverage by the mainstream media is important in Fourth Wave feminist organising as it allows for the scale of such events to grow, in turn, exponentially garnering more media attention. This then creates a dialogue between activists and authority by which structural and institutional changes can be considered.

However, in reviewing reports from the mainstream media – such as The Guardian, The Independent and – it is clear that little has been done to acknowledge the 5,000 women, transgender and non- binary people who attended the event. The turnout highlights the success and need for the protest event, which has been largely ignored in favour of headlines surrounding the controversy of the women's only protest (O'Connor, 2017; O'Reilly, 2018). Deducing from Angie Ng's comments on the SlutWalk Hong Kong protest in Protests as Events, this could be seen as a way in which the press has 'distanced the public from the movement' (Spracklen and Lamond, 2015: p 47). Much like the biased media reporting of Greenham Common Women's Peace Camp, the mainstream media have played an important role in the impacts of exclusion felt at the Statement Festival.

The Global North is currently experiencing an 'age of protest' (Clarke, 2015; Kauffman, 2018), in which women and other oppressed communities are becoming more comfortable with speaking out against injustice. The location of the Statement

Festival is relevant in this context as Sweden has always been at the forefront of gender equality legislation. Therefore, the illegality of the festival has set a precedent for future women's only events in Sweden, which will change the landscape of these events. This speaks to our nuanced, complex understanding of the gender spectrum in Fourth Wave feminism.

Disabled women have been somewhat overlooked in the organising of the Statement Festival. No information on accessibility could be gleaned from the Statement Festival website, therefore an email was sent to the festival organisers by the author (appendix three). The response to this email (appendix four) showed an awareness of issues arising from disabilities and highlights their accordance with Swedish law. However, it did not demonstrate an acute awareness of disability issues within intersectionality framework. It is somewhat challenging to assess the level of accessibility and inclusion of women with disabilities with no access to first-hand accounts of the event. Thus, the only assessment that can be made is that the impact of exclusion on disabled women attending the Statement Festival could have been limited by the organisers providing a range of options for disabled women, such as virtual tours of the festival site or live streaming the event. Live streaming would also provide an alternative for working class women who have been indirectly excluded by the price of the tickets.

Statement Festival can be likened to the lesbian separatist festival; Michigan Womyn's Music Festival. This comparison has been drawn from both events' "women only" aspect, however, their differences will now be critically evaluated in order to demonstrate a shift in attitudes and approach to women's only protest since Second Wave feminism. Separatist feminism, which advocates for the total separation of men and women, was a clear driving force for the Michigan Womyn's Music Festival which stated that the festival was only open to 'womyn-born womyn'. The Michigan Womyn's Music Festival ran from 1976 until 2015 after calls for the festival to shut down over their use of transphobic language (Ballou and Kilian, 2015). In contrast, the Statement Festival has certainly been a trailblazer for transgender inclusion in women's only protest events. By explicitly including trans women and non-binary people in the event, the Statement Festival has not only created a safe space for these people, but also highlighted an enhanced understanding of gender since the founding of the Michigan Womyn's Music Festival.

Another reason for the opposition of women's only events in Fourth Wave feminism is that they could be seen to perpetuate the stereotype of "weak women" who are susceptible to men who are all "predators". The more that women speak out against issues such as sexual assault in mixed gender spaces, the more that men will be given the chance to acknowledge their collective wrongdoings. This conflicts with Emma Knyckare's rationale for hosting the women's only festival, 'we'll run until ALL men have learned how to behave themselves' (Statement Festival, 2018).

The perception of gender in the Global North has shifted tremendously since 1960, from looking at gender as a binary construct typically linked to sex, to now understanding it to be a spectrum of gender identities formed as part of a social construct with no correlation to biological sex. The explicit inclusion of transgender and non-binary people at the Statement Festival, 'the world's first major music festival for women, non-binary and transgender only!' (Statement Festival, 2018), indicates a new perspective, and heightened acceptance of gender non-conforming people in the Global North. Juxtaposed with women's only events in Second Wave feminism, the inclusion of trans women and non-binary people at the Statement Festival was clearly expressed and welcomed. This created a safe space for transgender women which is an important factor in erasing the impact of exclusion at women's only protest events.

Radical feminists have been traditionally opposed to the inclusion of transgender women in women's only events as they claim that transgender people reinforce sexist gender roles (Davis, 2015). One radical feminist who opposes transgender people is British sociologist Carol Riddell, who commented in 1972 that transgender people, gay men and lesbians were 'the casualties of a gender role system that performs important functions for capitalism' (Taylor and Taylor, 1973). These outdated attitudes impact transgender people at women's only protest events negatively and add to the creation of an exclusive environment. However, it is important to note that while the radical feminist movement is ordinarily synonymous with transphobia, not all radical feminists are TERFs (Trans Exclusionary Radical Feminists). Self-proclaimed radical feminist Catherine MacKinnon spoke out for transgender rights in 2015, stating that 'Anybody who identifies as a woman, wants to be a woman, is going around being a woman, as far as I'm concerned, is a woman' (MacKinnon, 2015). Since the Second Wave of feminism, views on gender as a binary construct have shifted to a more complex understanding of a spectrum of gender identities, which is not linked to biological sex. Although the Statement Festival may be categorised by some as an example of radical feminism, it's explicit inclusion of transgender women and non-binary people help to make the festival a divergent approach to radical feminism and set a precedent for radical feminist events in Fourth Wave feminism.

Challenging the acceptance of transgender women at the Statement Festival, and focussing on the illegality of the event begs the question; if a nuanced and fluid understanding of gender has been expressed by the festival, why should it be only accessible to women?

Fourth Wave feminism comes with the understanding that gender is a fluid spectrum and accepts gender non-conforming people into the movement, therefore pushing the boundaries of what constitutes a women's only event. Due to this, in today's society, traditional women's only events have decreased in relevance as they do not represent Fourth Wave complex understandings of gender. The illegality of the Statement Festival highlights how women's only events promote exclusion and says a lot about our changing understandings of gender.

The findings of this chapter highlight a more fluid understanding of gender in Fourth Wave feminism, this has limited the impact of exclusion felt by transgender women and non-binary people within women's only protest events. This is portrayed well by the Statement Festival as the explicit inclusion helped to create a safe space for transgender women and non-binary people.

Using rationale from Second Wave feminist events, this chapter also brought a need for more representation of disabled women's needs to the fore of intersectionality studies within Fourth Wave feminism. In order to combat indirect class exclusion, this book suggests that practical solutions using technology could challenge the way women's only protest events are consumed. For instance, live streaming of the festival could have limited the impacts of exclusion faced by poor women. Other avenues that could have been explored include; creating a pricing strategy for tickets which covers costs but also allows for higher earners to contribute proportionately, and even making sure your external vendors are pricing their offerings appropriately. Similarly, virtual tours of the festival site would have created a new inclusive dimension to the Statement Festival, as well as explicitly welcoming women with disabilities.

Conclusion

'We need diversity for representation, but actually sometimes it's about diversity of thought' (Francis-White, 2019).

The women's only protest events industry has celebrated considerable positive developments, with many milestones along the way; demonstrated by Greenham Common's efforts in engaging poor women with the protest, and the Statement Festival's express inclusion of transgender women – denoting a shift in the way gender is viewed in Fourth Wave feminism. However, there are opportunities for further enhancement of uplifting marginalised communities. This heightened level of awareness and inclusion will firstly, limit the impacts of exclusion, and secondly, provide a rationale for the continuation of women's only protest events.

This book set out to explore the factors which promote exclusion within women's only events. The results of the study have shown a more intersectional approach to women's only events by their organisers since 1960. In contrast, the impacts of institutional and structural 'othering' of women at the intersections of multiple inequalities have seemingly failed to decrease over time. These external factors, such as institutional state violence and economic discrimination, have been found to be somewhat out of the control of the events themselves. However, this book has also produced some recommendations for industry in order to limit the impact of exclusion in future women's only protest events.

The limitations of women's only protest events from a race perspective, suggest that a better understanding of struggles disproportionately faced by women of colour such as police brutality, high rates of incarceration, and joblessness, would lead to more widespread knowledge on how protest organisers can protect these women.

The findings of the contextual analysis were significant to the study in that they challenged popular notions of women's only protest events in Second Wave feminism. This chapter concluded that the hegemonic retelling of Second Wave feminist history towards white, middle-class, cisgender women is accountable for painting a picture of women's only protest events at this time being white-led, with the achievements of black and anti-racist feminism trailing behind. This was found to be not the case, with anti-racist feminism existing roughly along the same timeline as white feminism, in mixed gender organisations and other areas where gender equality was not the overarching goal, such as the women's only support group Mothers Alone Working. This new information indicates that a retelling of Second Wave feminist history was needed in order to avoid exclusion in future women's only protest events.

Through evaluating and analysing the respective roots of Greenham Common Women's Peace Camp and the Statement Festival, it can thus be suggested that macro factors of systematic and institutional oppression are the main contributors to a system in which women's only events have become commonplace. Exclusion at women's only protest events come mostly from external factors which disproportionately target women at the intersections of multiple inequalities.

Since 1960, it is clear that the boundaries of mainstream feminism have served as a tool for marginalisation. Will women's only protest events advance into the future? Given our understanding of a non-binary gender construct in Fourth Wave feminism, there are issues with wholly separating men from women. However, this study also suggests that the context of these women's only events give way to an open dialogue surrounding topics which disproportionately affect women. This is significant in that, if future events acknowledge intersectionality studies, the same could be achieved for these marginalised groups of women.

Unconscious bias has had an important role in the impacts of exclusion at women's only protest events. This study found that the impacts of unconscious biases, which are held within every person and stem from what is outside of our own consciousness, are far more widespread than conscious (explicit) bias. In order to avoid indirect exclusion, which often takes the form of lack of inclusion, there are a number of recommendations that could be carried forward into industry; Taking a holistic approach to inclusion, women's only protest events in the future could look to use technology in order to gain more widespread views. For example, offering virtual tours of galleries or festival sites to include women with disabilities, and reforming pricing strategies to include those from a lower socio-economic background.

References

Allen, E. (2018). *Returning the Gaze, with a Vengeance*. [online] The New York Review of Books. Available at: https://www.nybooks.com/daily/2018/07/08/returning-the-gaze-with-a-vengeance/ [Accessed 13 Jan. 2020].

Aschoff, N. (2016). *Feminism Against Capitalism*. [online] Jacobinmag.com. Available at: https://www.jacobinmag.com/2016/02/aschoff-socialism-feminism-clinton-sandberg-class-race-wage-gap-care-work-labor [Accessed 7 Feb. 2020].

Ballou, A. and Kilian, J. (2015). *Why the End of Michfest Is Good for Feminism: Two Activists Weigh In*. [online] Everyday Feminism. Available at: https://everydayfeminism.com/2015/07/end-michfest-good-for-feminism/ [Accessed 12 Feb. 2020].

Baxandall, R. (2001). *Re-Visioning the Women's Liberation Movement's Narrative: Early Second Wave African American Feminists*. Feminist Studies, 27(1).

Binard, F. (2017). The British Women's Liberation Movement in the 1970s: Redefining the Personal and the Political.

Bordo, S. and Heywood, L. (2009). *Unbearable weight. Berkeley*, Calif.: University California Press.

Bowleg, L. (2008). 'When Black + Lesbian + Woman ≠ Black Lesbian Woman: The Methodological Challenges of Qualitative and Quantitative Intersectionality Research'. *Sex Roles*, 59(5-6), pp.312-325.

Braden, A. (1999). *The wall between*. Knoxville: University of Tennessee Press.

Bunch, C. (1972). 'Lesbians In Revolt'. *The Furies: Lesbian/Feminist Monthly*, pp.8-9.

Butler, J. (1990). *Gender trouble: Feminism and the Subversion of Identity*. 1st ed. Routledge.

Cameron, D. (2002). *Feminism and linguistic theory. Houndmills*, Basingstoke: Palgrave, pp.162-173.

Cho, S., Crenshaw, K. and McCall, L. (2013). 'Toward a Field of Intersectionality Studies: Theory, Applications, and Praxis. Signs': *Journal of Women in Culture and Society*, 38(4), pp.785-810.

Chicago, J (2018). *Test Plates for The Dinner Table*, 1979. 'A Reckoning'. Miami: Institute of the Contemporary Arts Miami, 4 December 2018– 21 April 2019.

Clark, C. (2007). *#TrendingFeminism: The Impact of Digital Feminist Activism*. Ph.D. The George Washington University.

Clarke, J. (2015). *Maina Kiai: We are living in an age of protest*. [online] the Guardian. Available at: https://www.theguardian.com/global-development-professionals-network/2015/dec/23/maina-kiai-we-are-living-in-an-age-of-protest [Accessed 3 Feb. 2020].

Crenshaw, K. (2016). *The Urgency of Intersectionality*. [video] Available at:

https://www.ted.com/talks/kimberle_crenshaw_the
_urgency_of_intersectionality?language=en
[Accessed 27 Jan. 2020].

Daly, M. (1968). *The Church and the second sex*. Boston:
Beacon Press.

Davis, A. (2019). *Women, race and class*. S.I: Penguin.

Davis, D. (2015). 'Are Transgender Women Just
Reinforcing Sexist Stereotypes?'. [online] *Psychology
Today*. Available at:
https://www.psychologytoday.com/gb/blog/laugh-
cry-live/201509/are- transgender-women-just-
reinforcing-sexist-stereotypes [Accessed 3 Feb.
2020].

Desmond-Harris, J. (2017). *Doubts about inclusive feminism
have little to do with the Women's March. They're rooted in
history*. [online] Vox. Available at:
https://www.vox.com/identities/2017/1/25/14355
302/womens-march-feminism-intersectionality-
women-of-color-white-feminists [Accessed 27 Jan.
2020].

Dowsett, J. (2014). 'Feminism for Sale: Commodity
Feminism, Femininity, and Subjectivity'. *York Space
Institutional Repository*.

Duell, M. (2019). 'Extinction Rebellion mothers stage mass
breastfeeding.' [online] *Mail Online*. Available at:
https://www.dailymail.co.uk/news/article-
7554245/Extinction-Rebellion-mothers-stage-mass-
breastfeeding.html [Accessed 5 Feb. 2020].

Echols, A. (1997). *Daring to be bad*. Minneapolis [u.a.]: Univ.
of Minnesota Pr.

Ekins, R. and King, D. (2006). *The transgender phenomenon.* London: SAGE.

Emberley, J. and Landry, D. (1989). 'Coverage of Greenham and Greenham as *Coverage'. Feminist Studies*, [online] 15(3), p.485. Available at: https://www.jstor.org/stable/3177941?seq=2#meta data_info_tab_contents.

Evans, E. and Chamberlain, P. (2014). 'Critical Waves: Exploring Feminist Identity, Discourse and Praxis in Western Feminism'. *Social Movement Studies*, 14(4), pp.396-409.

Evans, S. (1979). *Personal Politics: The Roots of Women's Liberation in the Civil Rights Movement and the New Left.* New York: Vintage Books.

Extinction Rebellion. (2019). 'We hope that the police will soon join with the rebellion'. *Twitter*. [online]. 16 April. Available from: https://twitter.com/ExtinctionR/status/111821691 9843315713 [Accessed 2 February 2020].

Extinction Rebellion. (2020). *Home - Extinction Rebellion.* [online] Available at: https://rebellion.earth/ [Accessed 2 Feb 2020].

Francis-White, D. (2019). 152. *Late Night with Emma Thompson and Mindy Kaling.* The Guilty Feminist.

Frank, P. (2016). *8 Radical, Feminist Artists from the 1970s Who Shattered the Male Gaze.* [online]

Gaard, G. (2011). 'Ecofeminism Revisited: Rejecting Essentialism and Re-Placing Species in a Material Feminist Environmentalism'. *Feminist Formations*, 23(2), pp.26-53.

Garland-Thompson, R. (2005). 'Feminist Disability Studies'. *Signs.* 30(2), p1557-1587.

Grayzel, S. (2014). 'Changing lives: gender expectations and roles during and after World War One'. [online] *The British Library.* Available at: https://www.bl.uk/world-war one/articles/changing-lives-gender-expectations [Accessed 13 Jan. 2020]

Greer, G. (1970). *The female eunuch.* London: HarperCollins E-Books.

Hamilton, J. (2019). 'Poor and marginalised people bear the brunt of climate change'. [online] *Redpepper.org.uk.* Available at: https://www.redpepper.org.uk/poor-and-marginalised-people-bear-the-brunt-of-climate-change/ [Accessed 5 Jan. 2020].

Halpin, H. (2017). 'Swedish music festival cancelled for 2018 following rape and sexual assault reports'. [online] *TheJournal.ie.* Available at: https://www.thejournal.ie/bravalla-festival-cancelled-rape-sexual-assault-2018-3477017-Jul2017/ [Accessed 13 Feb. 2020].

Hayden, C. and King, M. (1965). *Sex and Caste.*

Hayden, C. and King, M. (1966). Sex and Caste. *Liberation Magazine.* [online] Available at: https://www.crmvet.org/docs/sexcaste.pdf [Accessed 4 Feb. 2020].

Hooton, C. (2018). ''Man-free' music festival found guilty of discrimination'. [online] *The Independent.* Available at: https://www.independent.co.uk/arts-entertainment/music/news/statement-festival-man-free-women-only-discrimination-ruling-a8690116.html [Accessed 9 Feb. 2020].

HuffPost. Available at: https://bit.ly/2vzGJyO [Accessed 1 Feb. 2020].

ITV News. (2019). *In Pictures: Mothers bring babies as Extinction Rebellion highlights climate plight on children.* [online] Available at: https://www.itv.com/news/2019-10-09/in-pictures-extinction-rebellion-highlights-climate-plight-of-todays-children/ [Accessed 5 Feb. 2020].

Jarvis, J. (2019). 'Mothers from XR hold 'feed in' protests outside political party HQs'.[online] *Evening Standard.* Available at: https://www.standard.co.uk/news/london/extinction-rebellion-mothers- climate-change-a4302081.html [Accessed 6 Jan. 2020].

Jorba, M. and Rodó-Zárate, M. (2019). 'Beyond Mutual Constitution: The Properties Framework for Intersectionality Studies'. *Signs: Journal of Women in Culture and Society*, 45(1), pp.175-200.

Josephy, A. (1999). *Red power. The American Indians' Fight for Freedom.* Lincoln: University of Nebraska Press, p.52.

Judah, H. (2019). 'Judy Chicago's extinction rebellion: 'I went face-to-face with a new horror''. [online] *the Guardian.* Available at: https://www.theguardian.com/artanddesign/2019/nov/27/judy-chicago-interview-extinction-rebellion [Accessed 5 Feb. 2020].

Katz, C. (2012). 'People in Poor Neighborhoods Breathe More Hazardous Particles'. [online] *Scientific American.* Available at:

https://www.scientificamerican.com/article/people-poor-neighborhoods-breate-more-hazardous-particles/ [Accessed 6 Jan. 2020].

Kauffman, L. (2018). 'We are living through a golden age of protest | LA Kauffman'. [online] *the Guardian*. Available at: https://www.theguardian.com/commentisfree/2018/may/06/protest-trump-direct-action-activism [Accessed 26 Jan. 2020].

Kelly, C. and Breinlinger, S. (1995). 'Identity and injustice: Exploring women's participation in collective action'. *Journal of Community & Applied Social Psychology*, [online] 5(1), pp.41-57. Available at: https://onlinelibrary.wiley.com/doi/abs/10.1002/casp.2450050104.

Laware, M. (2004). 'Circling the Missiles and Staining Them Red: Feminist Rhetorical Invention and Strategies of Resistance at the Women's Peace Camp at Greenham Common'. *NWSA Journal*, 16(3), pp.18-41.

Lee, T. (2007). 'Rethinking the Personal and the Political: Feminist Activism and Civic Engagement'. *Hypatia: A Journal of Feminist Philosophy*, 22(4), pp.163-179.

Lewis, L. (2014). 'You Ain't the ONLY Woman: The White Cis Grasp on Womanhood Is Failing'. [online] *EBONY*. Available at: https://www.ebony.com/news/you-aint-the-only-woman-the-white-cis-grasp-on-womanhood-is-failing-504/ [Accessed 9 Feb. 2020].

MacKinnon, C. (2015). 'Harm is harm, hello'. [online] *On Century Avenue*. Available at:

http://oncenturyavenue.org/2015/03/harm-is-harm-hello/ [Accessed 27 Jan. 2020].

McGarry, M., & Wasserman, F., (1998). *Becoming Visible: An Illustrated History of Lesbian and Gay Life in Twentieth-Century America*, Penguin Studio.

Moraga, C., Anzaldúa, G. and Morales, R. (1981). *This bridge called my back*. 1st ed. Persephone Press.

Morden, R and Ray (2019). 'Greenham Women Everywhere'. [Public Lecture]. *Winchester Discovery Centre*. 14 December.

Naples, N. (2012). 'Community Activism and Feminist Politics. *Hoboken*': Taylor and Francis, pp.38-39.

O'Connor, R. (2017). 'Swedish women-only music festival to take place 'until men learn how to behave themselves". [online] *The Independent*. Available at: https://www.independent.co.uk/arts-entertainment/music/news/women-only-music-festival-sweden-statement-rape-sexual-assault-men-behave-themselves-latest-a7985921.html

O'Reilly, L. (2019). 'New exhibition celebrates Greenham Common Women's Peace Camp'. [online] *Evening Standard*. Available at: https://www.standard.co.uk/news/uk/new-exhibition-celebrates-greenham-common-womens-peace-camp-the-1980s-predecessor-to-extinction-a4265601.html#comments [Accessed 3 Feb. 2020].

Phelan, S. (1993). '(Be)Coming Out: Lesbian Identity and Politics'. *Signs: Journal of Women in Culture and Society*, 18(4), pp.765-790.

Phillips, R. and Cree, V. (2014).' What does the 'Fourth Wave' Mean for Teaching Feminism in Twenty-First

Century Social Work?'. *Social Work Education*, 33(7), pp.930-943.

Pritlove, C., Juando-Prats, C., Ala-leppilampi, K. and Parsons, J. (2019). 'The good, the bad, and the ugly of implicit bias'. *The Lancet*, 393(10171), pp.502-504.

Rage, R (2019). *Undervalued Energetic Economy, 1999.* 'Still, I Rise'. Bristol: Arnolfini Gallery, 14 September – 15 December 2019.

Ray (2020). 'Email interview with author. 29th January. Secondary research: Allen, E. (2018). Returning the Gaze, with a Vengeance'. [online] *The New York Review of Books*. Available at: https://www.nybooks.com/daily/2018/07/08/retur ning-the-gaze-with-a-vengeance/ [Accessed 13 Jan. 2020].

Ristanovic, V. (2019). 'The Art Warriors of the Second Wave of Feminism', *the Untitled Magazine*. [online] Available at: https://untitled-magazine.com/the-art-warriors-of-the-second-wave-of-feminism/ [Accessed 30 Jan. 2020].

Roth, B. (2004). *Separate Roads to Feminism*, Cambridge University Press.

Ryan, B. (1992). 'Feminism and the Women's Movement'. *Hoboken*: Taylor and Francis.

Sandoval, C. (1991). 'U.S. Third World Feminism: The Theory and Method of Oppositional Consciousness in the Postmodern World'. *Genders*, [online] (10). Available at: https://www.utexaspressjournals.org/doi/abs/10.55 55/gen.1991.10.1?journalCode=gen [Accessed 1 Feb. 2020].

Shane, C. (2018). 'How Do We Move Beyond Commodified Feminism?'. [online] *Literary Hub*. Available at: https://lithub.com/how-do-we-move-beyond-commodified-feminism/ [Accessed 8 Feb. 2020].

Sharma, J. (2018). 'Girl power rules the runway as designers make bold statements'. [online] *South China Morning Post*. Available at: https://www.scmp.com/magazines/style/fashion beauty/article/2163067/metoo-and-timesup-era-girl-power-ruling-runway

Shibles, W. (1989). 'Radical feminism, humanism and women's studies'. *Innovative Higher Education*, 14(1), pp.35-47.

Shugar, D. (1995). *Separatism and women's community*. Lincoln: Univ. of Nebraska Press.

Smith, B. (1989). 'A Press of Our Own Kitchen Table: Women of Color Press'. *Frontiers: A Journal of Women Studies*, 10(3), p.11.

Snapes, L. (2018). 'Swedish women-only music festival found guilty of discrimination'. [online] *the Guardian*. Available at: https://www.theguardian.com/music/2018/dec/19/statement-swedish-women-only-music-festival-guilty-gender-discrimination [Accessed 11 Feb. 2020].

Snyder, R. (2008). 'What Is Third-Wave Feminism? A New Directions Essay'. *Signs: Journal of Women in Culture and Society*, 34(1), pp.175-196.

Spracklen, K. and Lamond, I. (2015). *Protests as events*. London [u.a.]: Rowman et Littlefield.

Springate, M. (2016). 'LGBTQ America: A Theme Study of Lesbian, Gay, Bisexual, Transgender, and Queer History'. *National Park Foundation*, [online] 1(1), p.4. Available at: https://www.nps.gov/subjects/lgbtqheritage/upload/lgbtqtheme-intersectionality.pdf [Accessed 27 Jan. 2020].

St John, G. (2008). 'Protestival: Global Days of Action and Carnivalized Politics in the Present'. *Social Movement Studies*, 7(2), pp.167-190.

Statement Festival. (2018). *Statement Festival FAQ - all the information you need!* [online] Available at: https://www.statementfestival.se/info-en/about-statement/faq-en/ [Accessed 11 November 2019]

Swartz, A. (2011). 'Women Artists in Revolution'. *Oxford Art Online*. [online] Available at: https://doi.org/10.1093/gao/9781884446054.article.T2214396 [Accessed 3 Feb. 2020].

Taylor, I. and Taylor, L. (1973). *Politics and Deviance: Papers from the National Deviancy Conference*. Harmondsworth: Penguin Books Ltd.

Taylor, K. (2019). 'Black Feminism and the Combahee River Collective'. *Monthly Review*, [online] 70(8), pp.1-19. Available at: https://monthlyreview.org/2019/01/01/black-feminism-and-the-combahee-river-collective/.

Taylor, V., Rupp, L. and Gamson, J. (2004), 'Performing protest: drag shows as tactical repertoire of the gay and lesbian movement', *Authority in Contention (Research in Social Movements, Conflicts and Change*, [online], Bingley, pp. 105-137. Available at:

https://www.emerald.com/insight/content/doi/10.
1016/S0163-786X(04)25005-4/full/html

The Deviant Developer (2020). 134 *Women Only Events are
Sexist*. [podcast] The Deviant Developer on the
Intellectual Dark Web. Available at:
https://open.spotify.com/episode/4hTZJsOruzN1
DtnOFHZPYx?si=0kvBS0b2SAS5PLDhSOjQ_A
[Accessed 26 Jan. 2020].

Thelocal.fr. (2019). *The shocking figures that show the fight for
women's rights in France is far from over*. [online]
Available at:
https://www.thelocal.fr/20190308/equality-
remains-elusive-in-france-on-internationals-womens-
day-2019 [Accessed 13 Feb. 2020].

Thompson, B. (2002). 'Multiracial Feminism: Recasting the
Chronology of Second Wave Feminism'. *Feminist
Studies*, 28(2).

Thornham, S. (2001). *Feminist theory and cultural studies*.
London: Arnold, p.170.

Tobias, S. (1998). *Faces of feminism*. Boulder, Colo.:
Westview.

Toledo, (1998), from Baxandall, R. (2001). Re-Visioning
the Women's Liberation Movement's Narrative:
Early Second Wave African American Feminists.
Feminist Studies, 27(1), 225–245.
https://doi.org/10.2307/3178460

Valk, A. (2010). *Radical sisters*. Urbana: University of Illinois
Press.

Weber, J. (2018). *Judy Chicago Responds to Criticisms About the
"Dinner Party"*. [online] Hyperallergic. Available at:
https://hyperallergic.com/455572/judy-chicago-

responds-to-criticisms-about-the-dinner-party [Accessed 1 Feb. 2020].

Wenzlaff, F., Briken, P. and Dekker, A. (2018). If there's a penis, it's most likely a man: Investigating the social construction of gender using eye tracking. *PLOS ONE*, 13(3)

West, G. and Blumberg, R. (1991). *Women and Social Protest.* New York: Oxford University Press.

Appendices

Caitlin Powell

Appendix One

Q1: Were there any special measures in place to ensure Black and minority ethnic women engaged with your efforts at Greenham? If so, what were they? If not, why not?

Ray: I don't think there were. I will give you the context of how the country was at that time by way of explanation and understanding. Racism was rife in the UK: racist, violent policing, violent fascists, BNP, National Front and there was a massive anti-racism movement with an element of white male violence in left.

Being white but Irish meant you were a target for arrest and violent abuse; Northern Ireland was occupied by British troops and in the Republic/Eire lesbians were leaving to live in England often to escape the church and it's child abuse.

We did not consider it essential to actually be at camp, on the common, to be a 'Greenham woman'. Greenham women are everywhere was a 'meme'. You did not even need to live in the UK, we were an internationalist movement. We worked partly to show solidarity with BAME women internationally.

I was living in the west country in rural areas and villages which were white monocultural with possibly no BAME people/families except in cities like Exeter and Plymouth. Many (white) lesbian mothers left these areas to live in Bristol and even there their children were bullied at school. Also, some mothers were having to go to court and losing their rights to keep their children. In cities like London, Manchester, Brighton, Southampton, Leeds, there were Greenham Women Everywhere groups who campaigned, held fundraisers and ran coaches for big weekend actions but I cannot really speak with authority on the racial mix of these.

Some black women did come to Greenham but were targeted by racist Police and MoD police. As I understand it BAME women also risking being alienated by their families and religious ethnic communities by crossing racial boundaries to work politically with white people in the UK. We understood the need for separatism; some of us were lesbian separatists.

Greenham women were crossing the boundaries between women's liberation, lesbian and gay rights, the peace movement, environmental protection and land rights all of which were national and international. These worlds did not intersect well; some feminists thought 'peace' did not have much to do with women's liberation, the peace movement found it hard to accept a women only peace movement and plenty of heterosexual peace activists wanted us lesbians to be invisible so as not to give the press another reason to dismiss us. We were vilified anyway.

We had some class and race analysis of the targeted recruitment of poor white and black men into the military because colonialism as in the arms trade and military occupations by western powers was part of our analysis as women for peace.

Black and other women came from Kings Cross women's centre to discuss our lack of black women and accuse us of racism, this was a big issue for the WLM at the time and still is, though I think less so. This caused a split which resulted in yellow gate women separating from all the other gates. I don't think it resulted in more BAME women coming to camp.

Our focus was on breaking the nuclear chain which was/is a global military complex. In the first years a Japanese woman lived (and died) at camp having moved from Hiroshima womens peace camp. We campaigned over the undersea nuclear tests the USA and France were doing in the Pacific. We paid for women from the islands involved in the Nuclear Free and Independent pacific to come to the UK, arranged speaking tours and hosted them. We named the human and environmental costs of the uranium mining in Namibia and Australia, on Aboriginal land.

We networked with Seneca Falls women' s peace camp where USA military were on Shoshone land; 1 went to the women's Pentagon Action in 1982. Women came from La Ragnatela women's peace camp at Comiso in Sicily and there were other women's camps in the UK like Menwith Hill,

Aldermaston and Porton Down which grew out of Greenham.

Q2. Were there any disabled women living at Greenham that you knew of? And were there any adjustments made in order for this to be possible?

    Ray: Again, l will give you some context: the common was rough terrain and we were squatters so we were very limited in terms of infrastructural adjustments; we constructed temporary shit pits for big actions with planks and tarps for wheelchair users, they only lasted until the bailiffs removed them.

    Many disabilities are invisible but deaf women signed and lip read so that was Ok until it got dark; there were only hand held torches no head torches like today, we filled oil lamps with paraffin (and as a result ate a lot of mud and charcoal.) It was not a case of us and them, we supported each other with creative solutions, women with mobility impairments know their own capabilities and we did what was possible to support them. If someone had arthritis, they did not need to get involved with handling knives, axes, it all got done and we usually had a few upright chairs and old sofas to sit on if the ground was hard to get up off.

Mental health problems are disabling but we had a better chance of supporting each other in this. We really did not want to get anyone sectioned and some women lived at Greenham when they were not 'in care', others avoided care at all by living at camp. It was hard when someone did not take their prescribed medications and might do something like set fire to the sofa in the middle of the night or disappear for days and then turn up at another gate. We did not report them.

Women of all ages could turn up 24/7 escaping violent home lives and in poor mental health; we had love, laughs and singing and private night watch conversations where we shared stories of violence and sexual abuse; we began to understand why we might have food issues, self-harm, anxiety; we screamed at the planes and released our anger. We threw gloop at the convoys, banged drums and pans, it was very therapeutic to give vent to our suppressed anger in these ways. We tried out herbs and massage and some went to the local yoga class to help with the anxiety of living at camp.

We wanted to be a safe place for women but bearing in mind the drunken vigilantes, violent evictions, police surveillance from both sides of the fence, war planes overhead and heavy military vehicles going in and out of the gates 24/7 you could say "'we will protect you" they say, but never have we been so endangered.

Q3. Were there women from a diverse range of class backgrounds at Greenham Common? What measures were put in place for poor women who wanted to protest at Greenham? (I am aware of the 'camp dole' which you spoke about at the event, could you perhaps expand on that please?)

Ray: My first response to this question is 'we were all poor!' because we lived at camp in dire and limited circumstances and we understood that just because a woman had a husband with a well- paid job that did not necessarily mean she had access to that money. However, there were lots of middle class women who had more time, cars and money to enable them to be involved. Regional groups hired coaches for big actions so a ticket was cheap

Class difference was apparent in terms of ability to speak at our meetings and with confidence to the press for example but we tried to not let the press isolate us by asking to speak to our 'leader' with the response 'we have no leaders here.' We spoke to them with more than one voice and there were working class women who had plenty to say. We argued, we tried to take it in turns to speak in our meetings but some of us never wanted to speak and that was respected.

The support of middle-class people was essential to our survival; they had cars and drove about to get water or take us to Newbury nick so we could sing and shout outside until arrestees were released. Greenham women were in court, on bail and in prison.

We received money from people all over the world with letters like 'my grandmother was a suffragette, l can only afford to send you £5 and my thanks for being so brave' or 'my Quaker group wish to support you and we have had a collection. We will visit you soon, what is best to bring you?'. We tried to reply to all these letters, it was a big job and was part of the work of being at camp that anyone could do even if they were only at camp for a few days. Letter writing was much more common than today.

Again, the social and economic context must be understood. In those days getting unemployment benefit was much easier than today; you only had to sign on once a fortnight and eventually we were able to sign on in Newbury and dole day for nfa (no fixed abode) was also market day. We had a food kitty we all put money into but not if you had no money. No one went hungry (unless we all did). Peace groups and CND (campaign for nuclear disarmament) members organised hot food runs during the times of daily evictions when it was impossible to cook; our fire pits were flooded and equipment was taken.

For a while, I and other bloo gate women rented houses in a village in Devon so we could sign on by post. The post mistress was a member of CND, so she let us cash each other's giros. We hitched to and from Newbury, as did women from all over the country.

When we had plenty of donations travel money was available. Mostly travel money was for getting to speaks, demos and feminist events where we fund raised and recruited. A lot of money donations went on printing and posting newsletters. Camp dole was available for anyone who was living at camp when we had plenty of donations, it was an item on meetings agendas. It may have been for a few weeks, like waiting for your unemployment benefit to be processed, or if you were unable to claim benefit because of being under age or having a hidden identity. At bloo gate there were two Canadian women who I think got camp dole.

Once at camp you did not need much. We could often live off donations which included blankets, clothes, tarps, paint, tents, books, firewood, sofas, cooking equipment, prams, food and alcohol. Clothes were fun, we cut them up, dressed up and gave each other haircuts.

During the miners' strike a van came from South Wales with coal for us and we gave them some of our donations, especially food for the miners wives running soup kitchens. There was a lot of solidarity with 'Women Against Pit Closures' especially from South Wales, the links from the original march across S Wales from RAF Brawdy remained. This solidarity was based on the attack on working class communities across the UK by the Thatcher government which was hell bent on destroying trade unionism. The police violence was part of our shared experience.

Q4. Was there an awareness/understanding of a non-binary gender spectrum and transgender identities at Greenham Common at this time? How have your personal understandings of gender shifted since Greenham?

Ray: We were interrogating and defying the confining definition of what a woman was (allowed to be) as in gender roles ascribed by thousands of years of pretty much global patriarchy. These roles varied slightly in different cultures but the word patriarchy covers them all. We were not prepared to conform to the socially accepted roles for women as heterosexual wife, mother, virgin, whore. Even if we were any of these things just by being Greenham women on some level we felt we were redefining the parameters.

Man leaves his family to join an army and kill people equals 'hero', woman leaves her family to be a peace activist equals 'bad mother' or wife leaves her husband to live with a bunch of dykes equals 'a disgraceful bitch.' We understood the difference between sex, sexuality and gender because our oppression is based on our sex, our biological function as mother, giver of life. Our environmentalism was also rooted in our understanding of the sacred earth as our mother, giver of life. The walk from RAF Brawdy to USAF Greenham Common was named 'Women for Life on Earth'.

By being or living on the common this understanding became visceral. We lived and identified closely with earth, fire, water, air and the natural world set against the killing power of men and their war machines. There was no escaping this duality and it was clearly defined by a nine-mile fence.

We were what is now referred to as 'earth protectors.' Some women were looking from a gender defined as social relations/power perspective and saw nukes through the lens of masculinized militarism - the arrogance of patriarchy (I am man, the destroyer of worlds); nuclear weapons as the ultimate phallic object etc; and also, women with a lot of other perspectives - there was no one line!!

Some of us (lesbians) were more butch, some more fem and everything else in between, this was our 'spectrum' and being at camp gave us a safe space to explore and experiment with appearance, demeanour, behaviour, language, sexuality. But we knew that our oppressions, lack of opportunity and equal pay was due to our sex which could be compounded by our class, race or disabilities.

I think the men who supported us, as husbands, peace campaigners, etc were also exploring their own ascribed gender roles by doing what we asked of them, like not visiting after during the hours of darkness.

My understanding of gender today has not shifted much but it is still a journey. It seems to me that girls and young women are now even more subjected by capitalisms need for consumers of fashion, feminine products and identity. It takes a large share of global resources and contributes to our environmental break down. Chemicals on our skin, hormones in our water and if you can't hack the trad fem id, if maybe you are a lesbian, there's a whole other load of chemical coshes to help you cope.

Q5. What role do you feel that political lesbianism had on Greenham? Do you think this shifted any views on sexuality at the time?

Ray: Yes, political lesbianism was part of the feminist interrogation of 'compulsory heterosexuality.' It challenged heterosexual women to extricate themselves from sexual and emotional ties to men and see how they changed on the inside and how they saw the men and other women on the outside differently. Being at Greenham was a place where you could do this more easily than in the mainstream world therefore the effect on Greenham was positive. Political lesbianism was part of the sexual and gender spectrum we were exploring and this was happening in the wider pop culture too. Grace Jones, Bowie, K D Lang, the list goes on. We had had the contraceptive pill for at least 10 years by then which had made it easier for heterosexual women to experiment with their sexuality so re-considering your sexual orientation was another way that we could explore our sexual liberation.

For some this exploration led to changing from het to bisexual, non-monogamous, lesbian, celibate and back. It got confusing at times! But whatever you were up to, stick around long enough and your bleeding would synchronise with the rest of us and you'd be giving your blood back to the earth.

We wanted to be a safe space for all women, heterosexual, bisexual, lesbian, transexual. In 1988 section 28 was passed and Greenham was a safe space for lesbians so there were disproportionately more lesbians than in the general population. Some heterosexual women could sometimes feel uncomfortable experiencing lesbianism not being hidden. Everything provided the opportunity to learn, be challenged, have dialogue.

Many mothers were involved because of their concern, alarm, despair at the prospect of nuclear war and the poisoning of the earth that the next generations faced. Women brought their children to big actions; indeed 'Scary Little Girls' Becca's mother took her to G'ham as a child and her memories of this have prompted her to create the 'Greenham Women Everywhere' archive. Others decided against having children because of it.

This was a theme the press could relate to; they 'feminised' us as opposed to the angry lesbian man haters. Personally, 1 found this annoying, reducing our activism to our function as mothers; 1 and many of us were there because of our concern over the destruction of nature and all creatures and plants which we saw as the arrogance of man, especially after the Chernobyl disaster.

You must know that Sarah Green gave birth at G'ham early on. Once the military started experimenting with low and other frequency radio waves as crowd control on us (and the squaddies at the gates) we asked women who were pregnant or planning a pregnancy to stay away. Our menstrual cycles were disrupted by this and some got bad headaches. Much later quite a few were diagnosed with thyroid problems which they think was a result of being exposed to this by being at camp for prolonged periods.

Appendix Two

Gates at Greenham Common Women's Peace Camp. Anecdotal evidence from Ray at *Greenham Women Everywhere event* (2019).

Yellow: Consciousness raising. Academic. Cultural hub.

Green: Vegan. No men. Wiccans.

Blue: Young. Northern. 'Party gate'. Anarchist.

Red: Anarchist

Turquoise: only existed for a short while.

Violet: 'write-off' gate. 'eating meat and shagging men'

Orange: Crèche. Lesbian co-parenting.

Appendix Three

Email sent to Statement Festival organisers by the author.

Hello,

I would like to know if there is accessibility for wheelchair users at this event please? Also what measures are taken in order for the event to be inclusive to people with hidden disabilities please?

Look forward to your reply,
Many thanks,

Caitlin Powell

Appendix Four

Reply sent by Statement Festival organisers – translated from Swedish.

Hi,

Our festival has accessibility for wheelchair and we are following the Swedish laws regarding people with disabilities.

Acknowledgements

Thank you to my tutor Cathy John for providing me with the tools I needed to tell the stories of marginalised women throughout history. Your endless insights, breadth of knowledge, and encouragement have pushed me to achieve something which, about three weeks ago, I didn't think was possible.

Thanks to my interviewee, Ray. It has been a joy to learn more about Greenham Common from you and thanks for telling me to go to the Still I Rise exhibition at the Arnolfini.

BOOM!

This book was originally submitted as a dissertation in partial fulfilment of the requirements of a Bachelor of Arts (Hons) degree in Creative Events Management at the Arts University, Bournemouth, in 2022.

A note about Boom Graduates

We propel graduates forward so they can make their mark on the world - we push the boundaries, share brilliant ideas and inspire possibility. We publish dissertations as books, presented gift-boxed at graduation ceremonies, delivering brand-new research to the world quicker than anyone else. We plant trees for every commissioned book sold, and give our Boom graduates the chance to profit-share from their brilliant ideas. Furthermore, we donate the majority of our profits to funding research and scholarship for disadvantaged students who wouldn't normally be able to attend university. Through academic excellence and environmental sustainability, *Boom Graduates* are changing the world.

We are Boom Graduates - an imprint of Boom Publications Ltd. We are a more-than-profit company, dedicating over half our profits to providing university scholarships for underprivileged students across the world. We aim to become the globe's biggest provider of such scholarships – and if like Caitlin, the author of this book, you'd also like to contribute to making the world a better place, please contact us: we publish monographs, edited books, and moreover our graduate series – Boom Graduates – are presented at graduation days across the world in archival, lined museum-quality presentation cases, engraved with the graduate's name and award.

Boom Publications are based at the Duncan of Jordanstone College of Art and Design, at the University of Dundee in Scotland. We were one of the winners of the 2022 Venture awards hosted by the Centre for Entrepreneurship, and have since been shortlisted for the Converge Challenge, a national award that brings together ambitious and creative thinkers with innovative ideas to work with industry experts to transform their ideas into sustainable companies operating in the commercial world. We are also climate conscious and work with agencies to plant a tree for each and every book commissioned, offsetting thousands of tonnes of carbon each year. Follow us on social media to watch our forest grow @boomgraduates.

Thank you for contributing by purchasing this book. Please visit our catalogues on www.boompublications.com.

Notes

154

Intersections: Exploring Exclusion within Women's Only Protest Events

www.ingramcontent.com/pod-product-compliance
Lightning Source LLC
Chambersburg PA
CBHW070940260726
48661CB00003B/1059